Light of Recognition

Light of Recognition

Poems by
Maria Brady-Smith

Zoe Press
Washington, Missouri
2009

Zoe Press
Washington, Missouri
63090

Cover Design by Matt Wilson
Cover Art by Laurel Smith
Photo by Gloria Attoun Bauermeister

Contact information:
mariabradysmith@gmail.com

ISBN 978-0-615-26530-8

For Mike-
guardian of my solitude

Introduction

I have written poetry since I was a young girl. Over the years, I have questioned myself unendingly about my compulsion to do so when there were so many other, seemingly more important things calling for my attention. But I wrote anyway, finding such satisfaction in words.

I have come to realize, with the encouragement and wisdom of good friends, that writing poetry is one way of expressing God's light within me.

The best I can hope for is that the spirit in these pages will touch the spirit in you. It's a ridiculously high hope, but it is what God calls me to do anyway.

Pace

Imagine the sound of a cloud
moving leisurely across the sky,

a pine tree's imperceptible growth
compelled by its longing for light,

a gentle rain's slow
slide down the pane,

the sigh
aligning body, mind, spirit.

This is the pace of noticing,
the pace of gratitude,
the pace of change,

the pace of creation.

Table of Contents

Light of Recognition

I carve out a space

Never giving myself over
Wholly,
Holding back this bit
Just for me.

Sure,
It seems futile.
Always,
Other people's problems
Seep into my space.

Where I gently,
Guiltily,
Move it back out.
Sorry, I say,
So sorry.

But on the inside
I know
That I'll continue to fight
For that undisturbed core
Because it means survival.

Letting it fill in
Would drown me.

They will keep trying.
I'll keep resisting.
It will never really be resolved.

This part of me
Is the heart of me
That God has given
To only me.

My gift back
Is to notice it,
Treasure and protect it,
Let it grow.

Now I share it with you
Like a giant smile
Of hope.

Spring

Let's fall in love again.
We'll unlock this closed house,
Open the windows,
And sweep complacency
From the corners.

We'll step out
Into this familiar garden.
Its been asleep,
Silent and forgotten,
This long and dismal winter.

Birds have returned,
With resounding lullaby,
And the sweet smell
Of last night's rain
Penetrates the musty air.

Let's fall in love again.
Spring's warm sun
Melts hard hearts,
Entices new buds to swell,
And assures abundance
Once more.

Home Again Soul

As a child
I thought my soul
Was an organ
That sat
In my breastless chest.

Pure,
As white as a cloud,
A cotton ball,
A baby blanket,
Downy soft,

A place where
The Holy Spirit dove
Could rest.

The bad news, of course,
Was sin,
Which stained the soul—
Its pristine formlessness
Soiled by iniquity.

Confession
Washed it clean again
While penance hung it out to dry.

Silly, childish misconception
And yet,

These days,
I think of soul again.
I've learned to cherish
That pure white space—
Hot house
For tender seedlings of the self,
Resting place once more
For the Holy Spirit.

Father

I

My dreams took years to comprehend your death.
Each night they found you
Sipping coffee in the hard kitchen chair
Lost in a book
Children's chaos somehow tuned out.
Your absence jolted me awake each morning.
How could I have forgotten?

Then I found you less frequently,
A voice in the background reminding me,
"This is only a dream, you know,
He's not really here."
Eventually your image disappeared completely,
The empty chair removed.

II

I know your absence more intimately
Than I ever knew your presence.
Quiet man descending into your basement office,
Your remote thoughts.

You were quantum physics,
Astronomy, metallurgy,
Complicated political theories.
You were classical piano,
Emily Dickinson.
You were unreachable brilliance.

It has been twenty years since you died
And still
I try to climb the intellectual peaks
Where I last saw you.

III

Half my genes code for question marks.
Who were you, who am I?
I look back for signs,
Retrace the paths of my childhood
And my mother's home
For glimpses of you.

There is only one photograph of us.
I am shirtless, about three years old,
Sitting on your shoulder.
We are both smiling,
But I look anxious,
Waiting to be set down.

I sift through your piano music,
Looking for something familiar.
There is Bach, Chopin, Beethoven,
But one worn piece catches my eye,
Shumann's *Scenes from Childhood.*

IV

I remember your year-long dying.
"My father's got cancer," I told my friends
And waited for the explosion of comforting words.

But you bore it in silence,
Each new assault endured.
Dressing changes, indignities of exposure,
Slow draining of life,
Hopes deflated by test after test.

It was Mom you watched,
Patient with her reluctant surrender
To inevitable loss,
Teaching her what she'd need to know—
Finances, small home repairs,
Arranging ways for her to fill
The oncoming empty hours,
Down to the detail of a Christmas gift
For the holiday you knew
You would not live to see.

V

You died in private,
Your family dining in the next room.
Mom said she felt your spirit
Hover over the table that night.
Having said your good-byes,
Knowing we'd be alright,
You carefully closed the circle
And slipped quietly away.

It's in your death that I find
What eluded me in your life.
Silence was your way.
In a world too full of noise,
Silence is how you live in me.

Sorrow

Old sorrows waken at new sorrow's birth.
Forgotten losses stir their weary heads,
As disenchantments sigh and shift their girth.
Each death emerges from its settled bed.

They come from hiding places new and old,
Returning to the mind and heart…and throat,
As if by some familiar cry they're called
And, unexplained, the tears on which they float.

With tenderness, surrounding heart's new wound,
They lean to lend strange comfort now and sing.
As through the rain is heard their mournful tune—
A gift that only sorrows known can bring.

They gather up the babe and take her home,
A silent landscape back to which they roam.

Rocks

My husband
Brings home rocks
And sets them,
Like a treasure,
In the middle of the table.

I don't know what to do
With all of them.
They are interesting,
Most of them, to look at,
But numerous,
And not a part
Of the decorating plan.

There are photographs,
Sculptures and paintings,
Books and clocks—
And rocks.

I set them along edges,
In window sills,
Line them up on the porch.

And when I think
I've taken care
Of all of them,

He brings home another,
Fascinated and proud
And sets it
In the middle of the table.

The Broken Body Pushes On—

He, with a limp from an age-old accident,
She, with a scar from a cancer removed,
She, worn down by the war within,
He, with a tremor, nerves unraveled by pain.

Each bearing and carrying
The accumulated wounds
Of life and love

Compelled to move forward,
Driven by the hope of goodness
Planted deep inside
That shines

All the more luminous,
All the more lovely
Out of a body broken.

Catering Weddings

Filling water glasses,
Removing plates,
Moving,
In my black and white,
Colorless among them.
Occasionally someone tries to be
Friendly, solicitous.
I smile my brick-wall smile
And move on.

Here
I am the invisible observer.
I watch bride and groom,
Brand new in-laws,
Deduce their stories
From the way he glances sideways
As he lifts his wine glass
To his mouth,
The way the best man hugs her
Just a moment too long,
The mother of the bride's voice
Twitters an octave high
Like a nervous bird.

I work diligently among them,
Fascinated at how
This luxuriously expensive evening
Deteriorates into
Wine stained pastel silk.
Always there is someone
Worth keeping an eye on,
Always there is a story
Unraveling itself
To a silent and watchful
Servant girl.

Vacation Prayer

I know
That terrible things
Can happen any time, Lord.
But please
Don't let them happen
Now.

Keep my children safe
And happy.
Let us relax
For a little while
Together.

Let this warm sun
Continue to shine.
Let there be enough
Food and conversation
And silence
To go around.

Let us rest, Lord,
On this early spring weekend.
Keep cruelty away
For now.
Let there be enough, Lord,
Let there be enough.

Expect

She wasn't a great singer
But she was young and original
And gutsy.

She stood in front of the crowd
In the tiny coffee house
Banging on her guitar
And belting it out.

My favorite part, though,
Was when she finished—
The last strum

And then silence.

Then she looked up at us,
Expectant eyes
And a half smile…

Waiting.

Like a child
Who is accustomed to applause,
Who knows
She is the apple
Of her parent's eye.

I thought,
That's just the kind of love
You have to trust
To get from that awkward stage
Of potential
To the next stage—
Talent.

To me, though,
She was endearing
Just the way she was.

Journaling

In the same notebook
that I dump
the darkest toxins
of my soul,
I also create my dreams—
white lilies unfolding,
tender yellow stamens,
that too strong a breeze,
too hot a sun
could wilt.

All these thoughts
seem to lie together,
back to back,
if not peacefully,
then at least
without one destroying the other
because when my pen
drops off in sleep
and then morning comes,
the notebook still lies,
undisturbed,
on the floor beside my bed,
as if it has slept
as contentedly
as I.

Lesson

It is raining.
A young man and woman
Get out of a car
And head toward
An office building.
Ducking her head
Against the storm,
She runs by him
And grabs his hand.
He takes a few quick steps
To keep up with her
And then slows down
As if he suddenly realized
This was not somewhere
He wanted to go.
He allows her to pull at his weight
Until she decides to let go.

A year later, they are married.

This scene plays itself out
Slowly
Over the next twelve years
Except this time,
When she finally lets go,
She has two children,
A broken heart,
A baffling debt
And little energy
For running.

Morning Minds

In the morning, I wake up
Mourning doves coo me awake—

With a list of tasks
A new day.

Running through my head.
I think I will sit

I had better get them written down
For a while

Before they disappear.
On the porch with my coffee

There are phone calls
And watch the green.

I need to make
It embraces me these mornings.

Most of them
Who am I today?

To people I don't necessarily
Where will the green

Want to talk to.
Lead me?

But I should.
Ahh,

I really should.
I wonder.

Wonder Lost

A child,
Born herself,
An observer,
Watches her world
With unique eyes,
Wondering, wondering.
As she grows,
She discovers within herself
A singular way of interacting.

She feeds a grasshopper grass,
She makes the dead moth a coffin
From kleenex and flower petals.
She draws and draws
The beautiful pictures
That come into her head.
She knows a God
That I never taught her
Because I do not see so clearly.
She waits patiently
For Him to hand her the hopes
That give her courage.

Scared of monsters,
She magically shrinks them
To fit in her hand.
She throws the bad ones away,
Keeping the nice ones for friends.
I try to give her direction
But often I am awed
By what she already knows.

She grows a little older
And it is time to go to school
Where expectations change.
There is no time for her to think
Of what the colorful construction paper
Wants to become
Because an adult stands in front of her
Directing her to put the red on white
To make an American Flag.
She stares at the numbers through tears,
Wondering how to make sense of them.
It is as if she has landed,
Ker-plunk,

On some distant planet
Where she can no longer
Find her smooth path.
She is exposed to evaluation,
A mirror set in front of her
Revealing only her faults,
And shame at the realization
That she is different
From these other ones.

She recoils like a snail
Inside her shell,
But we demand that she come out.
She fights this new world
By kicking and screaming at me.
Seeing that I don't change it,
She mourns
That gentle world where she could unfold.

Over the years she slowly relents,
Realizing that
This is a monster she cannot shrink.
She learns to perform,
Making approval her goal.

Her heart is not in it, though.
It is as if, every day,
She is trying to interpret a language
That she does not care about or understand.

I find her sometimes in her room
Staring out the window.
"What are you doing?" I ask.
"Nothing," she replies, blankly.
I think maybe she is looking
For someone she left behind
Yet can't quite remember.

Chickens

These chickens
Walk purposefully
Around the yard,
As if they are going somewhere.
But they aren't going anywhere.

There is no place to go.

One finds a little something.
The others scurry over
To see what's up.
Nothing in particular,
But they are excited anyway.

At the end of a long day
Of wandering and pecking
They curl up together
In the straw.

Somehow, they seem to understand
That this is the best it gets—
Heartbeat to heartbeat
Resting in each other's softness
Comforted by
Their communal warmth.

I don't know that I really understand forgiveness

Survival—yes,
I get that.

Survival is holding onto the ship that I am
Until the storm subsides.
If I can weather it all without much damage,
Then I can let go, move forward,
Leave rocky waters behind.

But sometimes the harm done
Leaves gashes
Where parts of me leak out.

What is forgiveness then,
I wonder,
As I patch my ship
Bit by bit,
Eye always on the calm waters,
The clear blue sky.

Whispered Wings

They've been here all along,
Their songs filling the air.
Hundreds of them,
Hidden in a parallel world
Among the trees.

Their presence
And our emerging
Awareness of them
Has borne in us
A quiet reverence.

Over time,
They've learned to trust us,
Crossing more often,
The barrier between us.

A rosy finch builds her nest
In a hanging heather plant
And four tiny eggs hatch there.
A couple of wrens inhabit
A homemade house.
Chickadees and sparrows
Take turns at the window feeder.
From the top of a redbud,
The cardinal gloriously
Calls in the day.
Mourning doves respond
With their sleepy lullaby.

Friends stopped by tonight.
Having drunk too much,
They are loud and rowdy,
Flicking cigarette butts
Onto the ground.

As I listen politely
To slurred talk
And drunken assumptions,
I feel my whispered wings
Spread and take flight
Finding cover
In the crook of an elm
Under a canopy of leaves
Under the clear, dark sky.

I write you a love poem

I write you a love poem.
I tear the page from my notebook,
Fold it into an airplane,
And send it to you.

Caught on the breeze,
It floats gently down,
Engulfed by the fire
That burns between us.

They don't matter anymore—
The words,
My companion.

It is the embers,
The ashes drifting,
The smoke rising
That become a part
Of the air we breathe.

Dolls

We always played with her dolls.
They were better than mine.
Each had the same
Perfectly round blinking eyes,
A look of perpetual surprise,
And the same pursed and pouty lips.
Each was overdressed
In the hypothetical costume
Of a different country.

Since they were her dolls,
She directed the play.
'Orphanage'
Was her favorite dramatic tragedy.
She was the poor, sweet orphan.
I was the cruel and miserly matron.

"Now, you tell me that
I have to go to bed
with no supper," she'd say.
I complied
Because I liked her dolls.

"Let's pretend that
you lock all the orphans in the closet.
I calm them down
by giving them
a crust of my stale bread
and telling them a bedtime story."

Eventually,
I got tired of playing
The abuser to her victim.

I stayed at home with my own
Scrubby, well-loved dolls,
Their matted, over-washed hair,
Their clothes
Cut from material scraps.

Years later,
I saw her on the street.
Mid-winter cold,
Her hooded coat
Was wrapped
Around a skeletal frame,
Her remote eyes, grave face
Shockingly emaciated.

I did not yet know the word,
Anorexia.
But I understood
That she had become
Her own victim,
Her own abuser.

Examining My Motives

At first glance I smile
At the altruistic sacrifice
I have made.

But standing beyond,
There is an insecure school girl
Aching for approval.

And beyond her,
A small child cries
Afraid of being abandoned
In the dark.

I look further
To see a mother bear
Lash out,
Protecting her young.

At last,
A starving timber wolf
Stares straight into the eyes
Of its challenger,
Standing over
Its still warm prey.

Explorer

I ride my tricycle
Through the front yard
And onto the sidewalk
That frames our block.
My brother
Climbs on the back
Shirtless and sweaty
Making downhills exciting
And uphills impossible.
He'll push then.

I remember the feel
Of the rusty handlebar,
The squeak of the tires
The broken rubber pedals
Digging into the arches
Of my feet.

Around the block
Was a journey
Around the world.
Those houses on the other side
Were as unfamiliar to us
As Budapest or Brazil.

I'd study each one,
Wondering what kind of people
Lived in such strange
And beautiful places.

Heaven

Maybe it's a place
like I see sometimes
in my dreams.

We are all children
about five years old
and we are playing
the way children
this age do—
with total abandon
in the moment.
Running, climbing,
light and exuberant,
happy just to be.

Reborn as the delight
of God's creation.

All the damage, the pain
sustained in the world
has melted away.
There is no child
kicking the dirt
along the sidelines,
none that stomps off,
pouting, no little girl,
thumb in her mouth,
watching hesitantly
from a distance.

Fears forgotten,
we live immersed
in the everlasting
moment
of play.

A small boy appears now
on the horizon.
He has just arrived,
but this place is not
unfamiliar to him.
It has always
lived in him.

As he watches,
some children run by
chasing a ball.
A laugh lights up
inside him,
and like wings,
carries him into play.

Fall

Outside,
It is as crisp as apples.
Green slips away,
Leaving behind a rusty brilliance.
Death poses as life
To give its last gift—
Beauty.

Inside,
I prepare for the cold and dark,
Not by storing food and fuel,
But by spreading a soft blanket,
Covering myself
With warmth and comfort.

The heart settles in,
Not discontent
With its calmer pace.

Silence

I examine
The depths of silence
Like one might venture deep
Into a forest.
Here I may encounter
Fear and darkness
But passing through these
I rest in beauty and light.

Cycle

As I go about my daily work,
A tragedy is repeating itself
Deep inside of me.

My body sends forth
A perfect egg
Into its faithfully prepared womb,

Where it waits,
Hopeful,
Ready to bloom into wholeness.

But its partner never shows.

And circumstances deteriorate.

My womb holds tight now
To its loss.
Its ache reverberates
Silently through my body.

Soon it will let go
And blood, like tears,
Will wash the unrealized away.

My body weeps
And recovers
And then begins again.

Month after month after month.

Only three times
In all these years of months
Has the ancient plan
Been fulfilled.
Three daughters born,
Their own tiny bodies
Carrying a treasure trove of eggs
Deep inside.

Years ago, my thinking mind
Stopped considering new babies.
But that which is deeper
Knows no reason.
It only sees life as good.
It only knows
To try again.

Kindergarten

I was one of those that wept,
my heart clinging
despondently to the past,
wept to see my mother
turn so easily to leave me,
wept at this stranger's kind effort,
how softly she spoke,
coaxing me into her classroom.

I wept for my younger brother,
now home,
and the bittersweet vision of him,
in his pajama bottoms,
lying alone before the television,
transfixed by Captain Kangaroo.

I wept for the children around me,
placing their hard metal lunchboxes
on the tiny cloakroom shelves,
for the rows of pegs
all exactly the same,
for the monkey bars
that would one day soon
burn blisters on my tender palms,
for the child in the corner,
absently stacking worn blocks,
for the smells of crayons
and floor wax and milk
and small wooden chairs.

I wept for the unnaturalness of it all,
wanting only to be home,
to watch my mother
wipe cereal from the table,
sweep floors, smooth beds,
to listen to her hum
soothingly through my day.

When?

I missed something—
an event, a passing perhaps,
a visitation.

I'm not sure when it happened,
if it was quick or slow,
but something has passed over me
when I was not aware.

I look in the mirror
and I am astonished
at how gently, yet remarkably
age has touched my face.
For though I am not old,
I am no longer young.

Invisible Tiger—
On the results of genetic testing for Huntington's Disease

You have been my companion
for over thirty years.
I have lived in fear of you,
Tried to ignore you,
And looked obsessively
For every sign of your striking
For years and years and years.

I watched you slowly attack my father
And now my sisters,
As we helplessly watch them fall,
Unable to stop you.

Who is next?
We all try not to wonder.

And yet,
I have been driven by your presence.
All of my decisions have been weighed
By your ability to destroy at any time.
You have kept me humble and focused.
You have taught me that joy and tragedy
Are intertwined.
They strengthen each other.
I have come to value my mind and body.
I have kept them strong in preparation
For the fight.

I brought three daughters into this world,
A huge risk,
But one that meant hope
Was stronger in me
Than you were.

And now,
With a simple blood test,
You are gone.
 I no longer hear
Your silent roar.

Joy and astonishment and celebration!
All the love that surrounds me
Rejoices with me.

And my daughters, my daughters!
I tell each of them proudly
That this particular tiger
Will never stalk them.
They will never feel
Your hot breath on their neck
As they try in vain
To protect their young.

Still,
I can't help but wonder
If this gift of a blood test
Has taken something away from them.

You have formed me.
Learning to live with you
Has made me strong,
That which was threatened
Has become a treasure.

I don't regret your presence,
I have learned to love you
In the strangest of ways.
But if it is your death or mine,
I am willing to bid you
Good-bye.

Nourish

Today I will serve
A feast to my family.
I will cook beautiful food
With intention
And serve it,
Like artwork,
Like abundance,
Like love,
On a platter.

And our various worlds
Will come together
For this meal.
They will eat,
And I will take them in,
Savoring
The we
And the each,
However they are now,
However we are,
Just glad for this moment.

Audience

I need one,
Sometimes pretend
I have one
And that it is you
Quietly watching me
Taking down the story
Of my life
So that one day
I can see myself
Through your eyes
Which, I pray,
Are gentler
Than my own.

Midlife Crisis

is really only a crisis
if you stop and think
about the fact that your life
is halfway over
(more, really)
and you have spent so much
of the first part
either oblivious or obligated
or if you look
at your aging parents
and realize that there
are some parts of that
second half
that really suck,
like bodily pain and limitations
and Alzheimer's.

But if you keep busy
and don't think about this stuff,
why, I'm sure
you'd never wake up
in the middle of the night
to grab your notebook and pen
and head into the bathroom
where you can turn on the light
and write a poem
before your head explodes.

Winter Poem

In a field
There is a green snake.
He lies across a smooth rock
In the warm sun
Which is somewhere else,
Not here.

In that field
It is dry, dry.
Lichen flakes off that rock.

The snake is content
In the dry, warm sun
On the smooth rock
Somewhere else.

Here—
It is cold and dark.
Sheets of ice
Drop from the sky.
Cars fishtail
On the street
Outside my window.

I am content, too.
I lie, snakelike,
On this couch,
In and out of sleep,
Warming myself
With thoughts
Of other places.

50

Sledding

We walked that day
through falling snow,
dragging our sleds behind us.
Through cold wind,
into the heat of exertion
and beyond
to the perfect hill-
an abandoned roadbed,
gradual slope,
smooth curve,
half a mile long.

Caution is my mooring—
but not this day.
When we reached the top,
I stepped out front.

With running start, I flew
belly first onto my sled
and down the path.
I turned sharply,
dangerously close
to the forested edge,
then raced along the straightway,
smooth,
leaving my friends,
my thoughts,
my caution behind.

I became a breath
and the sound of my sled
surfacing the snow,
the whisper that drew me.

When the land grew level,
I slowed,
slowed
then stopped.

A stunning silence held me
a moment longer
before I lay back in the snow
looking up
into the dizzying flakes.

I closed my eyes,
felt my own breath,
my own heartbeat,
alone in the world.

If I lay long enough,
the flakes of snow would cover me
and I would disappear
into its whiteness.

Trespasser

There is an old woman
Who has made her home
In the corner of my mind.
She is shrunken, bitter,
Dark to the core.
She whispers in my ear
With her sour breath
Such ugly, disturbing things.

Her crooked eye peers out
And sees a mean, mean world,
Where no one can be trusted
And nothing is quite right.

She doesn't like the way I look,
She says I don't fit in.
Each time she spots a hopeful thought
She rushes over to sweep it out.
"Ridiculous," she scoffs,
"Impractical."

And just when I think I'll let go,
Maybe take a little risk,
She's standing there in front of me,
Arms folded and frowning,
Shaking her head.
"What will people think?"
She whispers.

I want her out.
She feels like death to me.
I point the way to the door,
But she refuses to go away.
"For your own good," she tells me.

"Just imagine what you'd be like
without me."

So I let her talk
And try not to listen,
But her voice drones on and on,
Drawing a blind
Of shame and caution
That no light can penetrate,
No song shine through.

Light of the World

An unexpected loss
Plunges her into a dark world.

So she writes,
Pulling from time and experience,
Every twig of hope
She can find.

She places them, by hand,
In a small brown notebook,
Arranging the words neatly,
Carefully, reading them
Again and again,
Thus blowing a spark of life
Into the pages.

See, she is telling
Whoever would listen,
Even in this darkness
There is beauty.

We warm ourselves by the flame
Of her words,
Drawn by the light
Of recognition.

Chemistry

I can almost see
The eyedropper of adrenaline
Being squeezed,
Drip by drip,
Splattering on my brain,
And sizzling there,
Dancing across the dendrites.

Anxiety
Jerks me alert,
Plays me like a marionette,
Rushes through my body.

It's just the panic response
Testing its equipment,
Always watchful,
Daring a disaster
To meet its well-rehearsed
Reaction.

House

I like this house
When it is quiet,
When I have time
To sit and think.

I think of this house
As a place that has breathed us
In and out all these years,
A silent witness to our days.

Tender sweetness,
Conflict and tears,
This house has absorbed it all
With fortifying patience.

It has stored in its walls
As I have stored in my heart
Each new moment
Of each unfolding day.

Yesterday

We had a dog yesterday.
Today we don't.

Sick beyond repair,
She left our lives
As sweetly
As she'd entered.

Her hair still sticks
To the bottom of my socks.
Her food bowls
Are soaking in the sink.
I don't know
What I will do with them
Once they are clean.

The backyard gate
Stands agape this morning.
No need to latch it now.

I will miss her most
On mornings like this one—
Her silly little dance,
Challenging me to play.
I throw her a treat instead.

When I sit down,
She jumps onto my lap
And tries to lick my face.

I don't like my face licked,
I tell her.
She yawns at me
And settles down

For coffee and a book.
Little heartbeat on my thighs,
Head hanging over my knees,
As if to say,
Oh, well,
I'll try again tomorrow.

Tomorrow is here,
But she is not.

Bye-bye, Bella.
I loved you well,
But never so perfectly
As you loved me.

Teacher's Dream

We were expecting
A snow storm,
Four to six inches predicted…
Hanging from the trees,
Covering the ground,
And especially,
The roads,
No longer negotiable.

That phone would ring
At six-thirty,
A heavenly voice
Announcing that school
Had been cancelled.

And suddenly,
Everything would feel calm
And exciting at the same time,
The day,
An empty white slate before us.

Instead,
We woke to a dusting,
The rooftops dappled,
Grass poking through,
And the roads…
Just dark and wet,
Cars flying past.

An ordinary day,
Made more so,
By the dream of snow.

Getting Away

He stands
On shaky ground,
Wishing he could steady himself
With some conviction
That what he does for a living
Is right.
He can't be sure,
And yet,
He's given himself to it.
Not all at one time,
But little by little,
Out of fear,
Needing to feed his family,
Needing to feed his image
Of success.

And now
That he's tied into it,
There's the matter of these doubts.
He dreams of being chased
Down endless streets.
He dreams of getting away
For a while.
What if he just had time to think?
There is no time,
Only pressure.

And so he drinks,
Because he deserves to,
It's the only way he knows
To get away,
To slow this trembling ground
On which he stands.

Basement

Rusty lunchbox,
Gaudy glass bowl,
Dusty picnic basket,
Dormant holiday decorations,
Broken appliances,
Half empty paint cans,
An unfinished sewing project
Calling out,
"Someday, someday."

Layers of old things
Covered with gray
Dryer lint and cobwebs and mold
And whatever it is
That seeps through
The cracked concrete floor.

Dank smells—
Mildew and dog urine,
Laundry soap and something chemical.
The odor
Of failure and loss
And unwillingness to let go.

In the basement,
I store old dreams
I don't know what to do with,
The baggage I just can't throw away.

This basement
Is the part of my story
Hidden from the daylight
Of a fresh and airy upstairs
That paints a more comfortable,
More intentional picture
Of who I am.

Beside Still Water

She lay in the nursing home bed,
clean white sheet folded across her chest,
hands intertwined, a gold ring on her bent finger,
delicate paper thin skin taut over bone,
bruises that need not heal now,
pale face so still,
thin white hair brushed back toward the pillow,
so simple a body whose spirit is elsewhere.

We've come to say good-bye
to my friend's grandmother.
I'm only here to comfort,
feeling a little like an intruder on a sacred moment.
I did not know her well, only stories and
the beautiful ripples of her life,
her children, grandchildren, great grandchildren.

We pray. Ceremony seems necessary.
I call awkwardly on God
thanking Him for this good life now finished,
ask Him to welcome His daughter home,
open the doors of eternity for this sweet soul.

We ask the nurse to search for a Bible
then recite the twenty third psalm together—
make her to lie down in green pastures,
beside the still water, restoreth her soul,
goodness and mercy have followed her,
she will dwell in the house of the Lord forever.
Then our voices blend in Amazing Grace.
Like a final lullaby,
I think we want to sing her into release.

I close my eyes and picture her
walking into the joy we only glimpse here,
joy she has not known
since her husband's death, she's felt
unnaturally alone, too old to adjust to change.
Now a familiar hand reaches out for hers.

I look over her head at daffodils
in a jar on the bedside table,
the only color in the room, a promise of new life
in the gray world of March.

Made in the USA